Brilliant Activities for

Creative Writing, Year 4

Activities for Developing Writing Composition Skills

Irene Yates

Brilliant
PUBLICATIONS

We hope you and your pupils enjoy using the ideas in this book. Brilliant Publications publishes many other books to help primary school teachers. To find out more details on all of our titles, including those listed below, please log onto our website: www.brilliantpublications.co.uk.

Other books in the Brilliant Activities for Creative Writing Series

Year 1   978-0-85747-463-6
Year 2   978-0-85747-464-3
Year 3   978-0-85747-465-0
Year 4   978-0-85747-466-7
Year 5   978-0-85747-467-4
Year 6   978-0-85747-468-1

Boost Creative Writing Series – Planning Sheets to Support Writers (Especially SEN Pupils)

Years 1–2   978-1-78317-058-6
Years 3–4   978-1-78317-059-3
Years 5–6   978-1-78317-060-9

Brilliant Activities for Reading Comprehension Series

Year 1   978-1-78317-070-8
Year 2   978-1-78317-071-5
Year 3   978-1-78317-072-2
Year 4   978-1-78317-073-9
Year 5   978-1-78317-074-6
Year 6   978-1-78317-075-3

Published by Brilliant Publications
Unit 10
Sparrow Hall Farm
Edlesborough
Dunstable
Bedfordshire
LU6 2ES, UK

Email: info@brilliantpublications.co.uk
Website: www.brilliantpublications.co.uk
Tel: 01525 222292

The name Brilliant Publications and the logo are registered trademarks.

Written by Irene Yates
Illustrated by Carol Jonas
Front cover illustration by Carol Jonas

© Text Irene Yates 2014
© Design Brilliant Publications 2014

Printed ISBN 978-0-85747-466-7
e-book ISBN 978-0-85747-473-5
First printed and published in the UK in 2014

The right of Irene Yates to be identified as the author of this work has been asserted by herself in accordance with the Copyright, Designs and Patents Act 1988.

Contents

Introduction

The **Brilliant Activities for Creative Writing** series is designed to stimulate developing writers to access the National Curriculum Programmes of Study for writing composition.

Each book contains practice activities to assist pupils in understanding, revising and consolidating their skills in writing. The activities are structured to help each pupil to understand how to:
- write for a widening range of purposes and audiences
- organize ideas into coherent and grammatically correct sentences
- improve, and make progress in, their own writing
- increase their accuracy in the use of punctuation
- develop their knowledge and confidence in spelling
- use and enlarge their writing vocabulary
- write in different ways for different genres and types of text
- develop their own way with words

The sheets are structured but flexible so that they can be used alone or as follow-ons. The ideas on the sheets can all be used as a basis for more lessons for reinforcement purposes. Each book aims to offer:
- a range of familiar text forms
- a range of appropriate contexts
- opportunities to experiment with words drawn from language experience, literature and media
- opportunities to select vocabulary according to demands of activity
- use of proof-reading, checking and editing, sharing with peers
- encouragement to pupils to reflect upon their understanding of the writing process

Each activity is fully explained and the teacher tip boxes give hints and suggestions for making the most of them or for follow-up activities. No additional resources are necessary, other than writing implements and extra paper for more extended writing where it is appropriate. Children should be encouraged to talk about what they are going to write, prior to writing, with a partner, in groups or as a class. Discussing what they want to write, prior to doing so, will help them to structure their thoughts and ideas. Through careful questioning, adults can help children to develop their vocabulary and understanding of how language works.

Obviously, all of the activities would work well if the children are able to word process on a computer at some times – this would be an added bonus.

It is hoped that this series of books will encourage pupils to use their writing to reflect upon and monitor their own learning, to encourage them to read as writers and to write as readers and, more than anything else, to learn to write with joy.

Brilliant Activities for Creative Writing, Year 4
© Irene Yates and Brilliant Publications

Links to the curriculum

The sheets in **Brilliant Activities for Creative Writing** will help Year 4 pupils to develop their composition skills, as set out in the National Curriculum for England (2014).

Composition

The sheets in **Brilliant Activities for Creative Writing** help pupils to plan their writing, by providing a structured format for discussing and recording their ideas. Pupils should also be given the opportunity to read and discuss other pieces of writing, so that they learn from the structure, vocabulary and grammar.

Composing and rehearsing sentences orally, prior to writing, helps pupils to build a varied and rich vocabulary and encourages an increased range of sentence structures. Talking through what they want to say will also help pupils to become aware of when they should start a new paragraph. The Tip boxes at the bottom of each sheet provide starting points for discussions.

The activities support pupils in developing settings, characters and plot in their narrative writing. Those sheets focusing on non-narrative writing introduce the use of simple organizational devices such as headings and bullet points. The Planning sheets (pages 45–47) will help them to focus on the features particular to each type of writing.

When pupils have finished their writing, they should be encouraged to re-read and their work and to think about how it can be improved. Discussing their work with you and with other pupils will help them to assess the effectiveness of their own writing.

Reading their writing aloud helps children to see that their writing is valued. Encourage pupils to use appropriate intonation and to control the tone and volume so that the meaning is clear.

Vocabulary, grammar and punctuation

Many of the sheets can be used to reinforce children's understanding of grammar and punctuation, but this is not the primary purpose of the sheets. Many sheets contain Word boxes to encourage children to extend their range of vocabulary and prompt them to use new words in their writing.

The following sheets deal with particular grammar and punctuation points:

- Choose a character (page 8) – use of adjectives, third person voice and present tense
- What can you see? (page 13) – adjectives
- Create a helpful character (page 15) – using third person voice and past tense
- Starting with dialogue (page 18) – speech marks
- Start with a noun (page 19) – nouns, plurals
- Start with an abstract noun (page 20) – abstract nouns
- Pesky pronouns (page 21) – pronouns
- Amazing adjectives (page 22) – adjectives
- Varying verbs (page 23) – verb tenses
- Starting with an adverb (page 24) – adverbs
- 'How to make' poem (page 34) – metaphors
- What's going on here? (page 39) – using first person voice and past tense.
- What did he say? (page 40) – speech marks

Writing

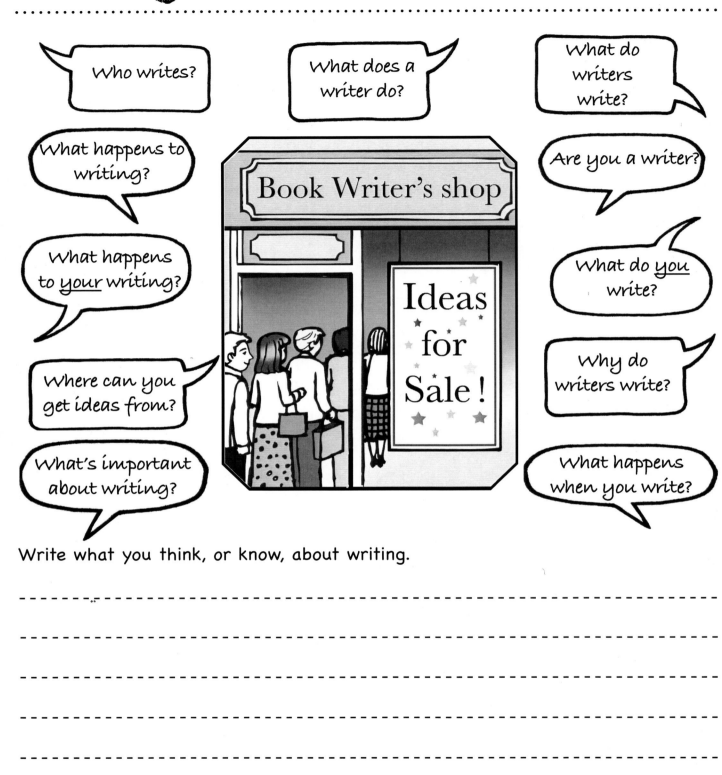

Write what you think, or know, about writing.

- -

- -

- -

- -

- -

- -

Discuss all the cues. Explore and develop ideas. Display note-taking of keywords so children remember and cue themselves in to writing the piece..

Brilliant Activities for Creative Writing, Year 4
© Irene Yates and Brilliant Publications

Drafting

Write about three things you can see from where you are seated right now. Don't worry about presentation, spelling or anything just yet! Just write.

A first draft can be as vague as you like.

First draft:

Now read through your piece and mark it yourself. Show where you need to change spellings, punctuation, words or even move bits around to make sense!

Second draft:

Stress how writers draft and redraft (many times) and that it doesn't matter what the first draft looks like, it's all about getting the meaning across.

Choose a character

Choose one of your favourite characters from a book, movie, comic strip, etc, and write a description of him or her. Tell us all about them. Give your reader a taste of why you have chosen this character.

Try:
Use some interesting adjectives. Write in the third person – he or she.
Write in the present tense.

Discuss what makes a character: not just a visual description but an insight into what kind of person the character is.

Brilliant Activities for Creative Writing, Year 4
© Irene Yates and Brilliant Publications

Create a character

Create a character of your own.

Base your ideas on a character you know well from real-life.

... or someone you have read about.

Ask these questions:

What does your character want more than anything else?

What would your character do to get that?

What if it all went wrong?

Write the story.

Discuss: What makes characters tick? Talk about the kind of conflicts which allow characters the chance to shine and win through.

Choose a story

My favourite story is ...

I like to watch ...

Become the main character in the story you choose. Instead of writing the story as he/she did ... , write the story as though YOU are going to do everything!

Title: _____   Character: _____

- -

- -

- -

- -

- -

- -

- -

- -

- -

- -

Try:
Understand why characters act the way they do and give explanations as though you are that person.

Re-cap on tense and pronouns. How does changing them affect the verb? Demonstrate with examples from books to hand.

Brilliant Activities for Creative Writing, Year 4
© Irene Yates and Brilliant Publications

Gathering ideas

Clustering is one way writers work on gathering ideas together. Start with one word on a page and just jot down anything that comes into your head. If you do this with an open mind, you will suddenly know what to write about.

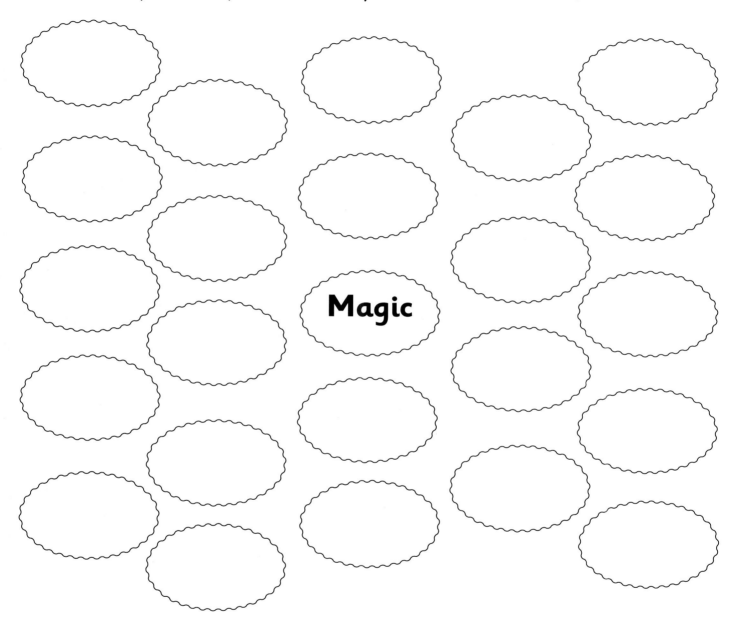

When you're ready just go! Write on another sheet of paper.

Remember:
Nothing you write down is **wrong**. Just keep jotting down words until an idea forms in your head, then write about it.

Practise this exercise frequently until the children can do it automatically without their conscious mind interrupting the flow. Encourage instant writing without judgement.

Win the vote

Write a letter to your group leader/teacher in which you're going to say why you should be chosen as team captain. 'Persuade' your teacher that you are the right person for the job!

Dear

- -

- -

- -

- -

- -

- -

- -

Yours sincerely

Remember:
State clearly the reason for your letter. Put forward precise arguments for why you would make a good captain and give examples where possible. Write in the present tense. Use scrap paper to write a draft.

Word box
believe
enough
mention
promise
therefore
group

Talk about the qualities that make a good leader/captain. Focus on the emotive and powerful feel of writing to persuade. Expect each argument to have reasons, examples and/or evidence to support case.

Brilliant Activities for Creative Writing, Year 4
© Irene Yates and Brilliant Publications

What can you see?

I see this all the time, but I can't remember ...

Look up from where you are sitting. Jot down five things you can see.

Look back down. Now write a detailed description of those items without looking back up at them.

Read and share your descriptions, then discuss them in the group.

Also:
Use a thesaurus to obtain lots of adjectives. Think of size, colour, use, texture smell, how you feel about it, etc.

Do a quick recap on description and adjectives. Often, we have trouble describing familiar objects or people; because we know them too well we never think about the detail.

Senses

Stay exactly where you are and write down a list of:
1. something you can see
2. something you can hear
3. something you can touch

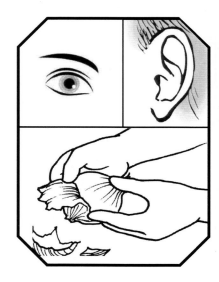

You might have three different things or an all-in-one thing.

Now transport your 'thing' into a different place, sometime in the future and write your story beginning ...

I knew something was wrong when ...

Try:
Get your setting written clearly so that your reader knows exactly where your imagined place is and what your imagined time is.

Word box
earth
different
arrived
natural
strange
thought

Use this opportunity to focus on listening skills.

Brilliant Activities for Creative Writing, Year 4
© Irene Yates and Brilliant Publications

Create a helpful character

Write a description of your helpful character here.

Tell, then write a good-deed-going-wrong story with your character as the do-gooder.

- -

- -

- -

- -

- -

- -

- -

- -

- -

- -

Try:
Make your story funny if you can. Write in the past tense and the third person (he was, she went).

Lots of discussion to explore the idea of good deeds and things that could go wrong. Talk about the resulting chaos.

Gold medal

What would you like to come first in/at? What would it feel like to win a gold medal? Imagine you have achieved your dream of the gold medal and you are coming home. Everybody is waiting to applaud you. Write the story.

Try:
Cluster all your ideas on scrap paper before you start. Write in the present tense, 'I am going home'.

Word box
Use some of these conjunctions:
if   and   because
since   when   but

Lots of discussion to explore and develop ideas before writing. Encourage 'clustering' to get the writing started.

Brilliant Activities for Creative Writing, Year 4
© Irene Yates and Brilliant Publications

Revise a story

Choose a story or another piece of writing that you have done recently. In order to edit and revise it, you have to read it and ask yourself questions about it. For example:

Can I make the characters stronger?

Can I make use of better adjectives?

Can I make use more active verbs?

Can I put any part into speech marks?

Can I turn any sentences around to make them more interesting?

Can I add to any part to make it more exciting?

Read the original story out loud to yourself or someone else. This will help you to find the pieces that need be changed.

Re-write your story here:

- -

- -

- -

- -

- -

- -

- -

- -

Try:
Re-read the new story out loud to see how successful it is.

Discuss the points of revision as given here. Stress that the focus is on the composition, not the spelling and punctuation at this point.

Starting with dialogue

Which is the most exciting start?

"Quick! Shut off the mega-volt-spike activator!" shouted Neevon.

or

It was the year 2088. The spaceship was racing towards Planet Zog …

If you start with exciting dialogue, you hook the reader straight into your story.

Try some dialogue starts here:

Remember:
To write direct speech (dialogue) you need to use speech marks at the beginning and end of whatever the character says.

Words for 'said'
shouted	whispered	cried
laughed	stated	screeched
wailed	declared	announced

Re-cap on the rules of speech punctuation. Explore, develop and demonstrate examples before writing. Share written work. Use starts for writing exercise.

Brilliant Activities for Creative Writing, Year 4
© Irene Yates and Brilliant Publications

Start with a noun

Which of these first sentences draws you into the story?

Fireworks exploded above the trees as the children watched.

Or

There were fireworks exploding above the trees as the children watched.

Write five story starts, beginning with a noun. You can make the noun singular or plural but it must be the very first word. (So no 'a', 'an' or 'the'.)

Choose one of your starts to carry on writing.

Remember:	**Try:**	**Examples of nouns**
A noun is the name of something. To turn singular nouns into plurals, you just add an 's', 'es' or 'ies'.	The noun could be the first word in a piece of dialogue.	puzzle book potato gnome puppy spider

Go through singular and plural rules. Lots of discussion about nouns as names of things.

Brilliant Activities for Creative Writing, Year 4
© Irene Yates and Brilliant Publications

This page may be photocopied for use by the purchasing institution only.
19

Start with an abstract noun

Some nouns are the names of things that you can't recognize by touch, smell, sound, taste or hearing. You only know them in your mind. These 'things' are called abstract.

Examples of these are:
> Excitement
> Panic
> Shame
> Determination
> Strength

List as many abstract nouns as you can.

Choose four of your abstract nouns and write a story start for each one. Share with your group.

Try:
Use your abstract noun to form headlines and then write a short paragraph discussing the subject of your headline.

Lots of talk and note taking about abstract nouns. Share the story starts aloud, and encourage comment and response.

Brilliant Activities for Creative Writing, Year 4
© Irene Yates and Brilliant Publications

Pesky pronouns

Pronouns take the place of nouns: I, me, he, she, her, him.

Write about a visit to a pizza restaurant when someone in your family group ate too much pizza and then no-one had any money to pay. Make the story really funny. Use as many of the pronouns as you can.

When you've finished, read your story through out loud to see if it makes sense. You may have to change some of the pronouns into nouns!

Try:
Get your imagination going by 'clustering' the word 'pizza'. Write in the past tense.

Words to help

ate	peculiar
separate	through
extreme	naughty
probably	

Re-cap on pronouns.

Amazing adjectives

Enormous, lumbering, elephants are not supposed to sit on mice. This one did!

The elephant sat on a mouse.

Which story starter gets your imagination working the most?

Write story starts for these three pictures. Begin your sentences with one or two adjectives.

1. _____

2. _____

3. _____

Choose one of the story starts to write the whole narrative.

Remember:
Adjectives are describing words that tell us lots about nouns.

Lots of examples of adjectives to be sure the concept is understood. Have a read aloud session for the story starts.

Brilliant Activities for Creative Writing, Year 4
© Irene Yates and Brilliant Publications

Varying verbs

When changing the tense of a verb, you sometimes have to change the middle and/or the ending of the word to make the sentence to make sense.

Start a story using one of these situations. Write four different beginnings, using each version of the verb. Can you think of another way of writing it as well?

To eat

He eats

He is eating

He ate

He was eating

To sing

She sings

She is singing

She sang

She was singing

To kick

- - - - - - - - - - - - - - -

- - - - - - - - - - - - - - -

- - - - - - - - - - - - - - -

- - - - - - - - - - - - - - -

- -

- -

- -

- -

- -

Try:
Find different verbs for the same actions. Use a thesaurus to help you.

Discuss the concept of 'tense' and the changes that have to happen to the verbs in order for the sentences to make sense.

Starting with an adverb

Adverbs tell you <u>How</u>, <u>When</u> or <u>Where</u> something is happening; for example: 'slowly', 'tomorrow', 'underneath'.

Look at this sentence:

<u>The boy ran quickly down the road to catch the bus.</u>

Instead of starting like this, you could start with the adverb:

<u>Quickly, the boy ran down the road to catch the bus.</u>

Using an adverb to start your sentences makes the reader take more notice.

Write six starter sentences making sure each one starts with an adverb. See if you can pull your reader in 'like a fish on a hook!'

Try:
Make your starter sentences so good that you need to write the rest of the story!

Word box
happily	inside	loudly
quickly	slowly	downstairs
towards	beyond	sadly

Take an adverb collection from the group to add to the help box.

Brilliant Activities for Creative Writing, Year 4
© Irene Yates and Brilliant Publications

All about 'Who?'

Pick one of your favourite stories, either from a film, book or TV programme.

Then choose one of its characters and write four facts about their personality.

Create a character of your own from four of the facts you like and write a fact file for your character.

When you have a really good character, create a villain to oppose your good character.

Remember:

All stories include characters of one form or another. Once you have worked out the good qualities of your character, try to think of a quality that might not be so good for them, that might cause problems for them. For instance, somebody may be too generous and end up giving away all of their money!

Have lots of books to hand for children to scan through and discuss personalities and qualities of known characters.

Major problem!

A story is always about a character who has a problem.

You need to get your character into hot water so that he/she/it can get out of it (eventually) by their own actions.

Choose your character and 'plunge' them into the worst problem you could ever imagine.

Word box

believe	peculiar	surprise
occasion	pressure	heard
different	experience	

Remember:
What usually happens in a story is that as the character tries to solve their problems, they tend to get worse. A villain or 'baddie' working in opposition to a good character can create a lot of trouble!

This should be how writers' stories start. Show the children that 'He woke up. He got up. He had his breakfast ...' etc is not necessary.

Brilliant Activities for Creative Writing, Year 4
© Irene Yates and Brilliant Publications

Describe your character

> Close your eyes. In your mind, draw a character for a story.

What does their face look like? Are they happy, sad, angry, aggressive, cheerful?

What is their appearance like? Are they scruffy or neat? Are their shoes always polished? Are they tall, short or bent?

How does your character move? Easily, with difficulty, gracefully or robotically?

Get your character clear in your mind, then write a description in full.

- -

- -

- -

- -

- -

- -

- -

Word box		
famous	favourite	popular
special	strength	important

- -

Try:
Look for good, strong words that describe, so use sharp adjectives and special verbs – eg don't write 'he walked', write he strolled, he shuffled or he bounded.

Have writers share their character descriptions with each other, make comments and respond. Then develop the characters further.

Storyboarding

Each box needs to a little rough sketch/picture with a few descriptive words.

A storyboard will help you plan a story..

1.	2.
3.	4.
5.	6.

Try:
Make a rough sketch in the boxes, then write your story from the ideas.

Using a storyboard helps with planning. Demonstrate one with whole group input.

Brilliant Activities for Creative Writing, Year 4
© Irene Yates and Brilliant Publications

Create a plot

A story or narrative needs a plot.

First pick your character ...

Give him/her a goal, something they desperately want to achieve. For example;

- to become a famous singer
- to learn to swim
- to invent a robot to clean their bedroom
- to finish their maths homework!

Now work out all the things that might STOP them achieving that goal.

My character is: _____

My character's goal is: _____

_____

These things will go wrong: _____

_____

_____

_____

Resolution: _____

_____

Now write the story.

Remember:
Do lots of thinking; discuss with your friend; think aloud. Get lots of ideas for 'trouble'.

Focus on having a good character to begin with who needs to achieve something, then everything goes wrong. The middle of the story is always where events take the character away from the main story line. Analyse stories known to the group.

Getting to the Wizards' Conference

Start with a title and the first instruction:

How to get to the Wizards' Conference

- Jump three times over the garden broom.

> You've been invited to the Wizards' Conference of the Year, but first you have to find out how to get there!

Try:

Think of magical ways to get there. Get all your instructions in the right order. Use scrap paper to note down important words. Write instructions in clear sentences. Use bullet points.

Focus on discussion. Lots of imaginative exploration and development of ideas and then writing down the instructions / directions clearly and concisely.

Brilliant Activities for Creative Writing, Year 4
© Irene Yates and Brilliant Publications

Acrostics

Henry

H andsome and smart
E ver so friendly
N ever caused any trouble at school
R eally, until
Y esterday.

> An acrostic is a simple form of poem.

Try these:

Friend

F _____
R _____
I _____
E _____
N _____
D _____

Rainforest

R _____
A _____
I _____
N _____
F _____
O _____
R _____
E _____
S _____
T _____

School

S _____
C _____
H _____
O _____
O _____
L _____

Help with vocabulary. Focus on the words being clear and concise.

Repeater poems

What I know

I know that ...
The sun shines,
The wind blows and
The rain falls, and

I know that ...
The

> You can make a poem work by giving it repeater lines.

Continue this poem writing 'I know that ... ' for every fourth line.

Write repeater poems using:
  I wish that ...
  or
  This is where ...
  or
  My Mum said ...

Try:
Make up some repeater lines of your own and write a page full of poems.

Discuss the example poem and use as a demonstration with whole group input. Give time for writing and read aloud responses.

Brilliant Activities for Creative Writing, Year 4
© Irene Yates and Brilliant Publications

Write a narrative poem

Write a narrative poem that gets through the school week, but things that happen are unexpected. For example, the first verse could be ...

On Monday, we made
Spaceships out of
Cornflakes boxes and we
Decided to go to the Moon.

On Tuesday, we landed and ...

Write the rest of this poem, ending it on Sunday.

Try:
Cluster lots of ideas of odd things that could happen in the poet's thoughts.

Encourage lots of creativity, using the 'right-side' of the brain, no criticism or judgement. Have a quick group talk to muster creativity.

'How to make' poem

Write your poem in the form of instructions.
For example:

How to make a perfect ...

girl   boy   pet
alien   monster   robot

Ingredients – You will need:

- -

- -

- -

Method –
This is what you do:
Mix and match with a magic spoon

- -

- -

- -

- -

- -

- -

- -

- -

How could I make the perfect little boy?

By mixing slugs and snails and puppy dogs' tails.

Try:
Think of more titles that could be fun to write about!

Lots of use of metaphors. Show how they can make this kind of poem really fun and interesting. Focus on imagination and expression.

Brilliant Activities for Creative Writing, Year 4
© Irene Yates and Brilliant Publications

10 ways to ...

I love writing list poems like this:

10 ways to be a good friend.

10 ways to get out of tidying my room.

10 ways to get out of doing homework.

10 ways to disguise myself.

10 ways to make a nuisance of yourself.

10 ways to cheer yourself up.

Choose a title and write your poem here.

- -

- -

- -

- -

- -

- -

- -

- -

- -

- -

Words to help
strange
question
remember
heard
decide
appear
caught
complete

Try:
Make your poem funny.

Lots of talk about titles to explore and develop ideas. The more titles suggested, the better.

Write a play

Start with dialogue between two people.

Who are these two people?
Where are they?
What happens next?

Try:
Give your scene a setting in the form of stage directions. Make sure the audience can understand what's going on when the script is read out.

Make sure pupils are familiar with a play script and how it's set out. Lots of talk about situation and what could happen. Write a scene and then act out in pairs or groups.

Make something happen

It was an ordinary playtime, and then ...

Write your story.

  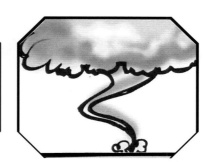 

Try:
Make your story as unusual as you possibly can. Use your imagination to come up with some really good ideas. Write it in the past tense.

Lots of discussion from picture, observations and 'what if ... ' scenarios. Focus on gathering ideas, planning and then writing. Share stories aloud for comment and response.

Making notes

Notes:
Jot down what you can see from the illustration above.

_ _

_ _

_ _

Now write down what might happen in your story.

Remember:
You do not have to write notes in sentences. The notes are just to jog your memory. Writing them as you go along is useful.

Explain about phrases and sentences. Explain about jotting down single words or parts of ideas. Use notes to start planning.

Brilliant Activities for Creative Writing, Year 4
© Irene Yates and Brilliant Publications

What's going on here?

Write the story.

Remember:
Write in the first person (I) and in the past tense.

Lots of talking to explore and develop ideas. Can be as silly as the children wish, without any restrictions or criticism.

What did he say?

Speech marks show when someone is talking. They are a bit like speech bubbles. Make up a conversation between two friends talking about what they are doing after school tonight.

Give them names and talk about their situation. Write what they say in the speech bubbles, then write it as direct speech.

Remember:
Use the speech marks for direct speech. Check punctuation!

Words to help
said   asked   answered
shouted   replied

Go through rules for direct speech punctuation. Have a discussion about what might be happening to generate ideas.

Brilliant Activities for Creative Writing, Year 4
© Irene Yates and Brilliant Publications

Beginning, middle and end

You know that a story has to have a beginning, middle and an end.

The beginning tells you about the setting/place/time and the characters involved. It introduces you to them.

The middle tells you what happens to the characters – usually a problem develops (some writers call the middle, *the muddle* because it's where things go wrong).

The end tells you how the problem is solved and how everything works out/ends up.

Think of a story you know well and split it into three parts.

Title: _____

Beginning: _____

_____

_____

Middle (or Muddle!): _____

_____

_____

End: _____

_____

_____

_____

Once the children grasp this, go through lots of stories you have shared to work out the beginning, middle and end.

Take one setting

Choose a place.

Choose a time. (Long ago in the past/far into the future/right now in the present time.)

Choose a character. For example, it could be an astronaut or alien, a snowman, a trapeze artist, a parrot, a footballer, a crab or even a frog!

Write what happens.

Remember:
Plan for a beginning, a middle and an end. Watch the tense of your verbs.

Recap on beginning, middle and end. Explain that the setting is in the stimulus of the story, so everything the writers choose after that must somehow fit into the setting.

How to make your writing better

Choose a piece of writing you have done recently.

Work in pairs to listen carefully and observantly, and to respond objectively.

Give three things your partner likes about the writing.

1. _____

2. _____

3. _____

Give three things you both agree would improve the writing.

1. _____

2. _____

3. _____

Edit your writing by:
- crossing out words you don't need
- adding words that you want
- changing words for better ones
- correcting spellings
- changing the order of words or sentences
- checking words in a dictionary or thesaurus

Get a review

Ask a friend to read your story and respond on this page.

The title of the story:

The author:

I like the story because:

The main character is:

The story makes you read on because:

The best bit of the story is:

Use this sheet for reviews of published stories as well as for group work response.

Brilliant Activities for Creative Writing, Year 4
© Irene Yates and Brilliant Publications

Plan for story writing

....

Title:

Setting:

Who?	When?

Where?	Why?

Add a problem. What?
(What goes wrong to cause trouble for the main character?)

Series of events to add to the problem:

1.

2.

3.

Resolution: How?
(How does the main character sort out the problem?)

What's changed? What has the main character learned from the experience?

Planning for recount writing

A recount can be real or imagined.

Title:

Setting:

Who?

When?

Where?

Why?

Events in time order:
What happened first?

And then?

And next?

..

After that?

And finally?

Bring your recount to a satisfactory conclusion:

Brilliant Activities for Creative Writing, Year 4
© Irene Yates and Brilliant Publications

Planning for persuasive writing

Title:

Introduction:
I am going to write about ...

Main idea:
I think that ...

Supporting point or argument:
I think ...

An example is ...

Supporting point or argument:
I think ...

An example is ...

Conclusion:
This is what I believe ...

because ...

All about my writing

Think about the writing you have done. Which kinds of writing do you enjoy the most?

What's the hardest thing about writing?

Think about the best pieces of writing you have done. What made them good?

Do you mind if other children and adults read your writing and comment upon it?

Does it help to talk about your writing before you start? Why?

In what ways has your writing improved?

How could you be helped to make your writing even better?

What changes do you make when you rewrite your work?

Brilliant Activities for Creative Writing, Year 4
© Irene Yates and Brilliant Publications

Thinking about my writing

Take a piece of your recent writing and make comments. Was the writing:

- mostly in the teacher's words?

- mostly in my own words?

- all in my own words?

Were the ideas:
- mostly from my teacher?

- mostly my own?

- all my own?

Did I:
- think it was OK, but was glad when it was finished?

- think it was good and didn't mind doing it?

- think it was great and really enjoyed doing it?

Have the children complete the questions before any discussion and explore ideas for making writing a satisfying activity.

Printed by BoD™in Norderstedt, Germany